OPEN BOOK IN WAYS OF WATER

Before you start to read this book, take this moment to think about making a donation to punctum books, an independent non-profit press

@ https://punctumbooks.com/support

If you're reading the e-book, you can click on the image below to go directly to our donations site. Any amount, no matter the size, is appreciated and will help us to keep our ship of fools afloat. Contributions from dedicated readers will also help us to keep our commons open and to cultivate new work that can't find a welcoming port elsewhere. Our adventure is not possible without your support.

Vive la Open Access.

Fig. 1. Detail from Hieronymus Bosch, *Ship of Fools* (1490–1500)

First published in 2023 by 3Ecologies Books/Immediations, an imprint of punctum books.
https://punctumbooks.com

ISBN-13: 978-1-68571-138-2 (print)
ISBN-13: 978-1-68571-139-9 (ePDF)

DOI: 10.53288/0454.1.00

LCCN: 2023939914
Library of Congress Cataloging Data is available from the Library of Congress

Book design: Hatim Eujayl and Vincent W.J. van Gerven Oei

Produced with the support of the City of Toronto through the Toronto Arts Council.

spontaneous acts of scholarly combustion

HIC SVNT MONSTRA

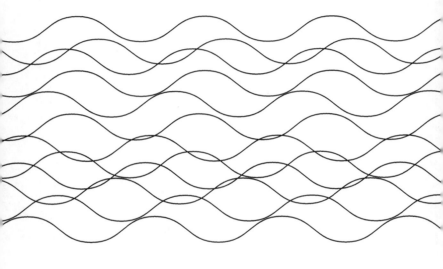

Adam   Wolfond

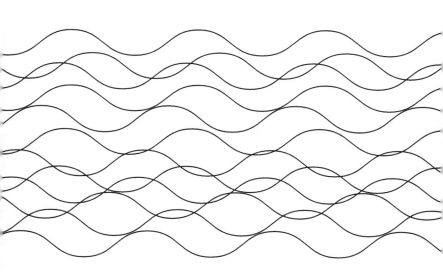

Open Book
in Ways of   Water

Contents

**Body of knowing is the relation of atmospheres
opening the language**

Have the ways of water the ways
of the rallying dances of people
                    no
because knowing is about
the ways of having paces
        that are landing and really fueling
Miss the ways
    that can feel games of space opening
the answers about autism
that are crafted by non autistic people,
and that means we know how to be in relation
with the paces of that world we talk about as
making beautiful again and I am same as that
world that is always coming and connecting
like some tears in my eyes will salt the earth
and the faces of people
    will turn toward it
        and the way of the questions
        will not be about autism
    but about sudden feeling
        and languaging that emerges
                will buttress as the body
            that moves.
                The way I want to talk
                is the way I really want
            to think about belonging
    but art's questions are using the ideas to feel
    the way I answer with my body and I can question
    the management of talking as the way of wanting sense
        but I sense that the way of knowing rallies
as dancing real dear inside easy giving body opens
        doors
        to
    needing
connection.

Opening

Erin Manning

Open book languaging the ways of water, autistic perception synaesthetically falling out of category before any
hardening onto fixed form can occur, water the force,
the current, the drip, the seepage, the push, the pull, the
accelerator, the reorientor.

Water paces the word, rhythms the path language needs
to pull itself out of the more-than of all that is still edge
and feel. But words are only one of the layers here, the
feeling-form of the path itself a character in this account
of how writing worlds. After all, it is movement, "inging,"
that is most at work here, agitating the sayable, taunting
that dreaded echolalia, the misunderstood unrefrained
force of impulse unrestrained. Inging, the movement of
language touching the flavor of its conduit, repetition-in-
rhythm. "[L]eurararara. I leurararara the water between
my fingers and easy is the dance." Through the syllables
we hear the echo, we dance the lalia.

How easy it is to return to a notion of language as
internal, as monologue, as mine alone. Neurotypical
training keeps us there, in an account of language devoid
of the activation contour that motors it. But language is
dance, and without pace it cannot find its way, its rhythm
disjointed. Worlds have to vector themselves into a shape
that languages. The way of water does a lot of this work
of pacing, pace as mode of existence of all that lives

between, of those atmospheres that only resonate in the synaesthetic ebullience of "rallying relation." But it is not only water that does the work of the rallying relation. Water is never only water. Water is the all-ways of flow, the inging of a million contours of movement-moving, and being moved. "Pace is in things and pace is patterning the ways I move and write."

That pace is "in" things shouldn't awaken archeological impulses. We are not talking about states, we are talking about movements. Pace pulses worlds into act, catching what most readily languages into its wide net. But to tone it, to tune it, to turn it toward the poesis of its rhythmic languaging, the relational web of facilitation must also tangle with it. Facilitation — the facilitation of facilitation — prods this parsing, condensing the flow into that step-by-step one-word-at-a-time we call language. At a cost. Because we must not forget the labor of the slow typing finger, working to locate the device's key, one long gesture at a time, elbow forward to keyboard, elbow back, elbow forward again, each activation its own complex challenge, facilitating hand on back, voice quietly confirming, encouraging. Be careful, though. It doesn't end here. What is facilitated is not simply the communication. What is facilitated is the rallying of relation. What is facilitated is the movement of worlds through the writing, beyond the writing. This is what we hear in the words, beneath the words. Writing worlds relation, the echo of the welter alive in all it leaves behind.

In the rallying relation adverbs proliferate, language's relational bend echoing with the unsayable quality of the more-than, that aspect of existence that cannot be reduced to me, to you. This minor sociality seeps through the line, reminding us that the facilitation of facilitation is never about how one person organizes another. It is about how the field of engagement teaches us to enter collectively in an activity of shared encounter. That language emerges here in a relational flow demonstrates the potent quality of a wording always in excess of the one-two. Facilitation lets the world in. "[T]he support I factually get feels like weight of magnetic fissures that line open thinking wanting the weight to help pace and slow running thoughts." In the magnetic force field there is both the quality of adherence and resistance, force-form in tensile push-pull. Thoughts ajumble, too quick to catch, too slow to parse, support becomes a way to carry both at once, in the relation.

"I am dark and heavy and feeling game of writing as real pressing pressure and although I am writing now I go to the dark floor of the sea to watch the way I am outside myself and yet inside the water." Inside-out, rhythmic pressure bubbles to the surface, become-word, become-world. Adam Wolfond lives here, his writing a magnetic reshaping of the forces of existence. The politics of this relentless shaping of language in the worlding are ever-present, the refusal to be constrained, to be framed, taut with feeling. Because the way of water is not a choice. It is mode of existence, life-way. The open lives here.

Well

The water I want to well is the deep language making meaning that deepens the way we think about autistic perception. The well is the way we rapaciously answer the way that neurotypicality speaks about arrangement of art attention and autistic importance that people don't really want and I think that the water is required for easy language and should not start to dry. The easy language thinks making the body and the world feel together and the way of the water moves into wanting cracks and management in words peoples and does not world. The people generally eulogize words toward meaning about peoples and things and I think words have laws that I don't obey. Language is moving and feeling and I think that pacing and verbing is always the way I see it. The way of language is the way I feel the words and the way I think about them as alive and the way open letters dance wanting words that language for pleasure. The way language moves thinking naming feelings so complex and I can't always describe the way I know it but I can tell how I dance with it.

Wet

I want to think about ball and the water to water the talking that unravels like wet yarn in saturation of lines rallying the way open directions do and the rally is more than the good people talking but the amazing expansion exiting the word meaning to be languaging that is autistic feeling like ways of water and I want you to want the way I wet the words. I wet words the open way. Open the words not to synthesize the water easy but think about the ways water and the world move to think about bathing the synaesthetic experience to walking waters of the words calligraphy ways with questions about what words about experience mean. I am thinking about the way people describe synaesthesia and opening the ideas about using the word towards the waters of thought and feeling that want more than words to describe them. I water the master's language to want more. The master's language wants laps around words that make seeing simple and I want waters of expression to answer eagerly and toward the way arts want worn experience rallying easy earnest questions to arrange autistic essay of easy fast understanding emanations of the waters. I am rallying a conversation about the salty words that art and literature talk about experience and I want the people to understand pace and perception always as the all ways questioning man in the center of every answer. The human thinks we

are thinking calmly wanting answers the anthropomor-
phic anthropocene. The man puts himself at the center of
words of meaning of all life and autistics always yearn for
more and deeper connections that suppers wanting synaesthesia as the main meal in reasoning towards all ways
wanting for the people to feel. Always appetite and thirst
for more understanding must swim in the synaesthetic
ways that waters come closest to describing.

Rhythm

I am going to write about the way of language as places of thinking and pooling wanting to always water steadier thoughts of weight and I wayfare the waters to vary so that is typing assembly towards a way of pacing the perfect cadence. The always typing is the way tough movement paces wanting the watching people wanting me to type on waters of fast rushing rivers to really race the rhythm. The rhythm thinks pacing as the wayfaring is always answering the calls of people and dance with the atmospheres of the different open places so I am easy to think about the ways I respond to the wanting talkers who inside the tribe of rallying speech are always thinking that typing arranges pace like wanting talking just knows what is in between the words when open wet words are languaging the landings like dinners overcooked but I think that I always am about the talking that doesn't need with words calming the body but the having the body calm the words. Old ways the language. Old ways are the long paths of walking that history paces over time to think nonlinearly about words and meaning but open knowing with the environment. I think that the ways of the waters are paces that move with atmospheres that pattern the rhythm and that walks idea the words and that always people want language to be still. I easy to eschew the people and I expect that people will try to read how I write as it is doing the hate of autistics liberating autistic language placing our way pacing into the way of perception and language I am all about and I am good at it and I know that people forget that I can write in my own language. My language liberates lines of neurotypical correction of my body and paced open language.

Pace

The pace is the atmospheres of movement that paces to gether and opens the ways I land perception and I question the way landings of words can pace more movement. Opening the pace thinks about how I language with things that I use and feel and I am some times wanting to hang on to pace of others' pacing so going to things is easy calming talking body to hear my pace and your ability to understand how peak of moments are to me patterns the words. I am thinking about giving objects the names of pace. I would write the toy as pattering fast talking patterning fast movement. Sticks would be called twallowing to the wanting ways of water. Of people I would say that pace would be called the yapping sound of dogs that manage to make me nervous. Loving logs that weigh yearning heavy setting near passing of wanting water instead. In the water is the movements and the weight that lands and moves and feels lines of easy waves of making language. Pace is in things and pace is patterning the ways I move and write. In the walks I see rallies of movement between things and I am landing easy steps languaging with the movement of atmospheres. I am pacing the energy always better than most because I see the wanting forest bathing in the wanting sun and offering wanting the easy way to relate without words and I see paces of wanting soul of the things to be part of rallying relation. I am going things to sand the time to think about living matter of things. You are the always butterfly object pacing to be always felt. The pace of the relation thinks across people and atmospheres and butterflies wave in making the feelings felt. You sometimes open the intensity of relation with doing waves in faster or slower paces making the intensity of language sometimes think in the ways of rallies. I want to same the way of pace and waves and weight and language and pattern is all about it.

Bathing

The bathing is about being immersed in water and the feeling of weight. Offering weight is the feeling of simple relaxation and the way my body needs to calm so the bathing is a weight of words too so I am feeling the weight of the world so I can move. In the weight I can land my thinking moving words so I gather them to water way the sentences I write. The bathing is the seeing of the words all at once wandering floating sinking and buoying feelings and rallying them together offers me writing pace with garnering navigational magnetic hand that feels the weight pacing the way fast typing thinks and the ways I think are fast wanting weight to slow them down. I see the making of words together managing the perception of them as packing together and I want the help pacing them so I can write my thinking down but language is also about my pace so old ways of writing are picking apart my meaning. In the navigation I am really trying to write using the pace and lines that most people use managing to grammar correctly but I am weakened bringing the right way of writing and the magnetic force of landing my words is the weight landing them going in sometimes different directions. The bathing in language is the easy feeling of the words questioning the many ways they dance. Easy rally is the calm way opening the waters of words to language game thinking people should learn to bathe and not approach language just as really demanding communication. The access to bathing and moving language is time and want for language to be like art. Language as art paces like dance between words and the partners change meanings. The bathing is movement of all things and art and atmospheres that pace together language is picking the partners but the feelings prance pace rocking the amazing thinking.

Stream

How is the stream languaging? I think that the stream is pacing man of autism's real insides of easy perfect thinking that does the calm flows of good important opening for easy times when writing is always a talking time of tired moves. I think that real time thinking is the streak of stream that for flows goes toward desire and old ways of the past that are already walked are naming thoughts before they flow. For the desire to flow one has to be the present moment of feeling and languaging is easy when it opens as the stream of movement toward. In the nothingness there is everything so rallying language is the changing and feeling streams of everything and nothing. Have the languages of others the calm dance making words so meaningful in easy relation because I find that English has limits like selecting words classifying want and what. Chinese language has symbols that connect and make relation. It easily for the stream relates because the stream collects feelings and objects and thoughts and languages world together. The stream also cataracts the names of things that memory can vary and it wants to move so it camps on the shore but memory is already past. The pace is the stream that allows for rally to always move onward carrying the language and memory making futures dance back and forth but always futuring the moment. I think that feelings are like the wind that we sometimes pay attention to and sometimes the wind moves us without realizing and that is the stream. The stream carries insides and outsides and they are making together the thinking and easy feeling that matters in my language. Using the way I move is the way I dance in language and the support I factually get feels like weight of magnetic fissures that line open thinking wanting the weight to help pace and slow running thoughts. Magnetic fissures pace tears in the pace of the autistic tic hesitating in the typing and like gravity settles the stream having eddies and pools. Find that gem of the fissure that dances pacing the stream to language thinking as thought happens.

Rain

The rain is the atmospheres of using ideas that really fall quickly and I am this person who rains on the words managing to sprout the seeds of meaning. The rain opens the clouds of talking opaquely and I think we all think we need more rain on the desert of making language dousing the dryness and languaging like ways of needing water to live. The rain is always the want of the earth to live and grow and going forging down so dance of rain is the days alive for me to think. Pacing like the rain is both fast and slow allowing me to go to good thinking and also allowing me to that calm place really rest and the way I need to be in my life. In my lit life I am wall of rain that spaces time for thinking and I am always about the time because the work and the world paces to it and I think that the world needs to care about different ways open rain times the space and the body. The work feels always timed to the pace of productivity and I am not wanting that I want the thankless actual time for thinking and asking about what language means if it sambas to the good rain.

Water Pace (Snake)

Knack to understand water pace is the watching of the surfaces that move image of and image in easy rally of atmospheres and the way the wistful wind and yes the easy earth in and under paces these movements. The skill for seeing movement is talking about my ability but the skill is always about the relation so the way rally wants to think always has to tail the way of the snake in the way of water and the way of the snake offers the thinking about shifting will of easy relation. The snake waters like waves and ripples and I think that the slithering thinks lustrous want dancing rallies of knack that is skill of the pace. In the way of the snake the actual movement undulates pace of the tail to the head and uses the wanting walk as the language I write as the languaging wanting the gathering amazing that snakes can think in movement and I think that they dance like water. The will is always the pace of the relation and in that I want to talk about the rally as the way we are always thinking and talking and making and feeling and rallying the way has to think about more than people but the art and the earth and the animals and the air and always tarring feathers of talking so I mean that we need to move the way we think about the rally-ing pace. The individual is not individual but about the collection in movement of arrangements that are danc-ing the rally and the way open ideas about individuality are should think about the will making sense with others and more than faces balking at desert of autism as the lack of will but the way we are willed by movements and feelings that makes us pace not just bantering humans. The making of meaning must not be permanent. Making must allow for finding it and making must feel the way finding easy rallies for relation.

Bubbles

The way of writing always thinks with bingeing bubbles. The way pace opens calm finding bubbles is the pop of pace talking in rally that presses the good floating thought for wanting meaning. The way of the language really flows through the many ways and the bubbles are going to the artful air of thinking and when they pop they splatter lines of thinking streams. I think that bubble pops are the naming other things about to answer but the spraying actual water languages more. I think it languages the way I feel about names of things and I want to be able to describe the way I think about words as always making easy thinking more complex by answering in open ways that gets people thinking about how I see words in wanting space that likes to wrap the very good meaning doing the notorious work of authorship but reads managing making the namings dance the way I see. The good bubble is thriving in the prism of colored movement and the varied pace of authoring the waters of soapy easy names suds the now of words about to bleed colors of thinking. Pace of the bubble finds the language of atmospheres and the assembly of the amazing meaning is about to pop to the sound of the same feeling as long easy pace. I'm place – change of itinerary of thoughts that before I had but now shift with the typing rhythm. The meaning I refer to is the way pace of the typing can be hard for hanging on to meaning before the bubble pops. I am languaging my direction. Languaging direction is more noticeable for typists because the words are slower than talkers who can cover up their shifts. The way open easy talkers talk names things wanting quick thinking to resolve the metered feeling. The cartoon bubbles are not the same as what I am referring to and my bubbles are bathing the language in waters of soapy kaleidoscopes of feeling.

Weight

I want to write that the weight of water opens my ability to swan dive into the world of sense and I can feel knowing as the wanting for more connection and opening that way is padding resistance to the incoming forge of feelings that persistently hand language of touch and I want to make soaking sense of it. I am having a part in the way I feel by always pacing the waves of intensity and I think that I need to wean right way other than just writing but I am scared to share the way my body moves because easy neurotypical people are always watching and naming autism as problem and I need to let people manage my movements to be included and that means that we manage to suppress a lot of good work by autistic imaginations and I want to be about imagination and not about easy explanation. I need to say that I want the world to understand that I am trying to watch everything and I want to say that autistic lives are pacing differently than the talkers who can move quickly and open the conversation to be more about the way we are fasting thankless time to bathe otherwise in the paces of autistics and I easily can talk about the weight of water as the coping mechanism and doing the immersive dance of the relation that neurotypicals ignore. In the way of weight as coping mechanism I think that we need to vary the landings of openness – world the way of water and the way of pace and the way of relation will change. The weight of water lands the body that I sometimes cannot feel and support is also helping me land this language and this is not the same as the management of autistics but is the way I can express in English but I am saying that there is more to movement than what most languages name and I want the world to use my words to think more about the way landings and pacings feel and the way autistic sense has my heart. To think that people are different should thankfully be exciting and I think that the work needs to be creative and open for new ideas to change the way autism is thought about and open your minds and bodies to name things as language possible for giving the autistics in the world a chance to shape it with our insights. Open the management the way autistics are telling you and think about having autistics share more of the ways we need support. People are languaging autism in letters of legislation and of that I need to say that people like me need to write it and open the conversation to have a better insight into bathing weight of sense and support. Open the weight to understand the sensory the support and the difference of weight of oppression that is often imposed on autistic people because the weight of support can calm and the weight of the restraint can cause harm and anxiousness. Interested in the calming loving sometimes feeling same peace in the way I am encouraged to express myself beyond words.

Springs

The springs dance the underland thoughts of rushing waters and they rupture the earth with fresh thinking and the making of new pace of mostly life that dives in. Go to the spring to water new thoughts and pace love of making changes to hard rock that motions toward the shape of water pacings and I think that the circular motion of underland and overland is like the deep understanding of what the people can see and not see so the way of the spring is like bathing in the waters of the unseen understanding. Underland rush of rich rivers dance and flood the caves of thought and understanding that is a way other people can think about me and how the autistic mind thinks without words alone but with movement. The rich meanings of mind and movement my body knows rallying the collection paces the means by which I am languaging. The pace is gaming the way of the movement so the pace becomes the language wanting portability to the way we think about communication and relation so I am wanting people to understand the language of the water with the earth. Love that body and earth are like art forms that can have so many meanings. Sometimes the springs are so full of hope that people forget that there is more underneath that we only get a glimpse of by the fissure the water breaks. Having the rain of water gushing through the fissure is like how

I gather the words feeling them rush through me and landing in a lake of fresh new paces and forms. The dance between the language and the movement is always the way to understand me and how I want people to think together because the relation in how people think with me is the way I am about to rally and I can't do it well if people expect me to talk or the writing will die.

Waterfall

Waters of thankful bodies of rallies such as pace of lasting languishing preening dancing of water falls. I want to water fall the way talkers do and I want to be able to talk like a gush of words but using the dance of support is like amazing synergy of thinking and I am eager to type with aided support that gushes language the autistic way of feeling. The waterfall the way using inside language that is the water density of heavy weight is like the answers that are demanded by the people who want answers and I want the languaging to fall pacing the ways of rare tumbling of the voices that are not heard. The waters that eagerly rush toward the edge think on the precipice of the feelings that are on the verge of being languaged and they are then talking lasting the way of the time that it takes waters to land typing is like the rush of feeling that I have to assemble and I need the weight in my thinking body to language people's way but expression is the way that waterfalls move. Real thinking is the tumbling rush the pace of the arts and the ideas that are perceived and the unconscious feelings that we are having to question away: can waterfalls easily understand everything that the family of thinking arranges or does the arrangement assemble after the water lands?

Hot Water

I think that heat moves molecules that are making paths of doors and thinks with the ways of writhing steaming tendrils of thankful divergence. The water that boils are like the letters that move in the dance of the patisserie that lands colors of easy food for thought. The making of heated water really requires the fire of desire for movement. Using the ways of fire is the way relation is about to think with the water that paces the making of the bubbles and the steam and the ways the good magic happens. Bathing in hot water is scalding but the language burns through me like the random letters roll. Pretty colors of words that land are the result of boiling the sugar and the food colorings that fall on the display of the patisserie. Long boils go toward the reduction of dense gravy but the language begins with open ingredients that people want for thinking and the ingredients can think more about how they want to assemble before they boil too long. The assembly paces depending on the relation between the ingredients and the making has the potential to be anything but the heat transforms that and the maker has to be mindful of rally between the ingredients and the dance of fire. The language cuts the meaning like the fire can destroy and the ingredients of language is the world. Language is better when pace is making it so the steaming tendrils are the possibilities paving the way. Have the people doing the language dance the lucky ways I have to think and feel the making? Open the ways to boil but not burn. Boil boil boil.

Dance of Calm Water

The dance of calm water is like the farming for band of partly patterns of all the ways of languaging paces that are calmly moving wanting the waves to get much energy from the shore of the making bathing like floating and I am like the buoy you use to forget how to say swim. The buoy faces the surface of the water and paces easily to the waves without taking me under. The way I want to talk thinks about how easy it is to float on the surface of language but I answer by going under the surface and that is when people want more easy explanations but I can't express myself as a surface talker. That is why I name languaging as the like for expression the way of the body and my gaming of the rally between people and the environment and I am thinking that talkers don't really understand important grit of autistic typing and movement. The farming for language partly is like the patterns we feel in the water that pace the rallying exchange in relation and that pattern I feel so much but I can't speak it I can only move to it wanting people to understand this way of communication big time dance thinks without talking. The farming lines are like plowed lines that pattern the pages of language in the field of forms and the water patterns languaging as pace. The buoy can be what carries me also like the fast tractor on the field but instead I rally on the same surface but game the deep waters of activity that are influencing how I need to language. Open water needs buttress of land like the way I am supported to type the way my body needs to language the depths to surface but the way patterns of my writing emerge always comes from the rallying pace. Pick the calm waters to understand the depths of activity that dance what you can't see.

Well

I want to write about the well that I use to understand language and how I learned to read on my own. Feeling I always think about when pace of letters is part of the well I use and the well is the way pulling the words easily I am thinking that the wanting well is the dance of the pace I pull in the way I master the rally. I am thinking that the well I use to describe my experience is lettering words that easily come to me like rain but fall in the well and pressing weight of the pulley is the weight of sentences I need to write and that is rallying the conversation and open words maybe are too easy to get lost in the way I talk about them but the words I learned to read when I was young were like rainbows of color and sound and the way that I learned to read was always about the way words danced. Good answer to the way I experience words as rallying dance is rivers of pace and wanting the finished sentences but I am easily distracted by the way language feels and that is all about the rainbows of letters that are inside the words bursting their languaged meanings. Go to the least tacky real thinking about how you experience music and that is how I feel and understand pace of words as communication and more than words because the pace is how each word in the sound makes a meaning bursting better than the word offering an experience of wanting and the language of meaning. Fast thinking is rushing my brain about the wells of rich words that gimble in rallying wave associating the pace with the meaning. The language must associate the music of movement that is the waters that assemble the patterns that surface and the naming has living baffling exciting ladders landing and falling and very much inviting us to climb.

Chlorinated Pool

I want to think about the simple pool pace of stillness
and the way words can float. The way language makes
a sentence is the way the words float on the surface of
meaning and the pool can be chlorinated water putting
the talking words face down in the deadness of distilled
preened purity. The chlorine is the name of the water
purifier that games with bacteria to leave the water and I
think of it as I remember the ways it stings my eyes and I
think that pattern of purity uses the same notion I think
about when people want answers about questions around
autistic perception. I think that I want to assemble things
and that is why the experience of stillness is the antith-
esis and the problem when language is presumed only
to be written or spoken because open words are pacing
things in the world and pace is the meaning of language.
I so much think that the way we language comes from
the movements we make and in that movement wean-
ing the meaning is like trying to get the bad bacteria out
of the water but the bacteria are the way life lives and
dies socially so the bacteria are the way open thinking
about people should move beyond the game of human
life as the most important. I use the metaphor to think
and that is easy when faces in the words rally like trying
to tress language in bows in the way game of social talking is bound to rules and that really is the tough part of

being autistic because those rules are so like the chlorine in the dead pool. Faces are slowly arriving to the words the way that life and color wears the person and that is how words are very alive but not restricted to the English language.

The Dance of Atmospheres and the Pace

I want to write about naming things and why the ways of water help explain things that move and vibrate and how on the water we surface. Good start would be to go to the water calm in disposition and I ramp in the feeling and I go to think about the dance the water has with the other elements and of the way I am answering. The way I am answering is going with the languaging of the wills rallying that have elemental characteristics like making getting longing patterns using the atmospheres and in that the way arrangements are about relation. I want to think about the easy way of thinking that goes nothing like the way we think by itself but how the easy relation talks to the want for bathing in the moment of moving and the wind will blow a certain way but the water languages the pattern of the wind in forgetting names for how it does it. Has the pace of the rain the answer to the thinking thunder and pace of the thinking clouds the pace of the warm and cold air and have we the pace of the atmospheres like the headaches that shape how we feel? Think thankfully that want for fascinating phenomena is fastly becoming a language because autistic management must think about the openness of the way we feel the atmospheres and I need people who in that understand that way going to the place having the most calm can help bathing to become a not painful experi-ence but a language of home and comfort. Management is the way most people care for autistics but support is calmly feeling the arrangements of the atmospheres that as autistic people many of us feel and to dance you know the way good relation moves when the partners can feel not only some of the body but the way the room feels and that opens the way to think about support as the dance of atmospheres.

Pace of the Undercurrents

I want to write about open places where surfaces are visible like lakes. The way the lake manages finding meaning is by the wind and the varied heaving undercurrents that are creating patterns on the surface of the water moving so that we have a sense of where the dancing relation comes from and how that easy art of movement is the making of meaning. The meaning is calm and always something of fantastic making miniscule changes of languaging paces that ways of liking my moving language must buttress the feeling reading. The way people should read my language should be lining the loving pace of gaming the movement to feel and paving making new inscribed lakes not paths of long gravel because the water can change quickly. Gaming the movement of my writing is to follow the curves and patterns that language with the changing fluid feelings and chilling out. The people answer so heavily by the meanings of words that they forget to follow the loving movements that do not make sense to them because it is making of sense through movement that opens the meaning.

Giving Water

I want to write a feeling of giving water. I want the water to quench the thirst for bathing in the dance knowing how feelings are wondering all the thinking and the dance is the very ace of gifting. The pace in the water is the gift I want to give the people and I want names of languaging patterns to tabulate the forms I think in making sense of the rally so that when people think about people dancing they always think about getting the feeling of watering destination fasting the pace and the way that the water isn't amalgamating the drastic fastness of talking. The ways I tabulate forms is by watching how the water is really rallying with the ways open atmospheres move so requisitioning a name for it is impossible. I am gaming the way the dance is leaving pace of destination that wants waters named. Rally the tension between the open bathing and the thinking to name and that is the thankless game we play but the water easily feels what bathing with dance knowing the ways having want really for being chill.

Watering Plants

Have the plants the green amazing leaves without rallying with the water? Green chlorophyll that the sun makes must rally with the water and the making is the chance of needing care like the way I same need the ease of the need the need for caring rallies that makes my pace knowing real love is germinating game in the make. Real chance is the landing of all the bringing of water and supper of ingredients pacing to gether at the right time and for that I make the rallying dance the chance for better paced life. Real people are made of water and powerful to dance the patterns of the flow of life if they pay attention for doing different languaging that opens the names of things like autism and needing the making of remembering that we are answering the ways of pathology when we need findings on feeling and family of care that think about resonance with the way plants think. The way language of plants works is with owing the ramifications of exchanging what makes for better life and sharing the earth's resources and the rally is the answering of breathing in of carbon dioxide and breathing out oxygen. Can want for life be able to survive if we were all the same? And can plants give you oxygen if they really were people? No because we need difference. Rallying is everything opening up the variability of making and that can change in the way the dance buttresses glowing man of autism's life and the dances bake the seeing the care the recreation the real way of support that bathes in the rallying ingredients of relation. The way of watering plants must consider the way long paces of elemental dances go or else the plants will die. Vary the way you can feel the long paces patterning the pulse of life.

Rain and the Catching Sweet Sounds of Walking Rain Drops

Rain in ready drops of thinking about the heat and the way the steam is released from the asphalt questions about what the street is wanting. The steam grows to meet the rain and the rush of traffic gears thinking to way the river's rush and the spring of wanting blooms towards dancing. Watching the people move in city space time that the rain interrupts and the breaking pace of weather opens another space questions inside the rhythms of plotting drops address themselves to wander. Easy to want to go outside the choir of full city space time but the music in the ways of rain and asphalt is a rally of imagining the ecosystem that brings good living to groups of living beings that belong. The easing inside relations that grow with city blocks the possibilities of space inside the composition wakes with the rain and the pools that flood the reasons to be always busy. Openings are weaving wanting into dancing days of rain.

Calm Water of Assembling

The assembling is a forgiving place of swamps that foster possibilities for easy open life. The swamps are lease for life that waters many species that can nurture the wanting ecosystem wanting more understanding about diversity. The landing of bathing is in jam with the life forms the freedom rally. The freedom rally sounds open like frogs and birds and bees and water amazing things you make the same answers for wanting diversity when you think of the swamp. The ways in which I think are always about life and love and having a heavy heart and pacing the ways peaceful rallies simply are about making loves of wanting the ways of diversity. Rallies that are political are offering peace but bitterness about addressing rights are competitive wanting the money to be controlled caving to business interests and we make some people answer to that and that makes swamp land less valuable but we are a bother to people and we autistics are land in the swamp. The value of that swamp is life sustaining so leave it alone as priceless. The dance of the swamp is the ways we also want to be together in the world so let us be. The ways leasing making life is languaging the way of meeting the ecosystem and I want the government to have more regard for looking after the swamps of life.

Tidal Waves

The tidal wave is the rally between the easy earth and the water and when the earthquake shakes the water rushes like a wall gaining speed and the waves destroy the people and the gears for society so talking can feel like that it can feel like destruction in rallying moments between the water and the ways it communicates with the ways of the easy earth using the power of making together. Like the thinking the tidal wave is powerful and it can sometimes shake the ways we put emphasis on the talking rally. Does good power come from the feeling of the easy earth or the talking person? I don't know but the ways of the water language the love flaunting the earth's power over us. Power is flaunting questions about the ways we play with ideas that are present right now and the ways of power can have the home of the watered earth offering life or the somethings of naming abstractions that don't have the bathing dance with the easy earth. Bathing of making life with the earth is different feeling than naming things in the world and I want people to know that I back home in the easy earth can bathe in it and family of making life is all around even in the destruction of the tidal wave. Language they say is power but having understanding in the making knowing in that easy earth is languaging life that are feelings of having the rally and knowing names of things and theory is not feeling.

In good thinking answers come from talking and feeling together so the words come in inspirations feeling the earth so I think there are both names and thinking feeling and having the emphasis on categories of things can be destructive to the rally. Pace of variability dances family of life so the dance uses different frequencies of making in the easy thinking feeling earth.

Living Is about Managing Support

Open world is always changing and that reality is what name of wars is about because sometimes we want stability and that doesn't exist in the ways that some of feeling can be sad about not really being with relation with the same loving person. I want to write about family of love that is like falling into maybe my teaching about water so is the way of water the way knowing the relation. Pace of that amazing water opens up the making of flow and change so the making in the relation is impermanent and the making messy connections is about calm adding to the good people for coming into my life. Pace of using sheer easy living is for me about starting support doing the dance initiation. It is that initiation that makes my living possible buttressing the bread of life and the starting support jumpstarts me and my ability to camp to game the sometimes feeling space that is making me feel calm. The amazing camp is temporary dwelling glad to dance with others but the home is really about moving to dance to really rest and the mother people talk about is home. The more I write the more having management of dancing calm is essential and really having the mom is good for that and I make managing of brave self think about brave buttressing mom living for me. The way managing the team happens has mom's making same work feeling fangs of pressure of the bad people who want to

put autistics into homes of incarceration and I manage in
knowing that I won't be in one.

The Thinking Seeing
Cutting Currents

I want to write about the leaking far game of the bad badass actual Adam that needs the always thinking time to bring water dance to the array of facing others that think I am talking about very ideas about autism and not about the waters in relation to who I am as an experiencing person about the real want for languaging as walking into the world like water moves. I am going to start a making of experience. Look to the sometimes calm water and I see much life like swimming for food easy pacing to the tide and that is how I manage mind thinking of dancing relation and bathing in the undulating movement that carries meaning. The ways I manage landing feelings is like the water that misses the amazing shore in the want to talk but I can think openly easily the ways in which the ticking tide dances the time of the earth and I see the movement so much that it is always exhausting to keep in rally go to the oxygen of the ways of amazing varied cutting currents and the game is the open easy rally. Pacing the language to the talking is difficult and thinking is easy so try to express experiencing the way the auras that lease the seeing eyes and that becomes rally of amazing atmospheres raining toward me. Gaming the ways in which the auras open the rally is like seeing layers laning the attention and that is trying to deep dive into the different cutting currents that need my attention of that I eagerly want to say that I go to the toys and the sticks to keep myself from thinking if I am talking too much about gaming the easy can of chatter of that I answer that I can easy see management of relation but in my eyes I see more.

Open People's Meek Thinking about Language

I want to focus my writing on language that people will think about easily dancing the way of water I am thinking about time and how people don't want to dance. I am good at pacing my own way and I question the way language orders with experience. To always rain language I am very curious how the talkers can language answers and to sometimes speak so quickly. I youthful and thinking person am so ready to need the answers that are questions inside me. People are always asking why I am not always speaking the way they do and that is sometimes hard to answer and I want to language in speaking tools bearing the weight of the world's questions I with people can be intimidated. It is talking that would name easily the way management is going toward speech and that really is the question not the way the man of autism languages and languaging as the typing movement that can bathe in the atmospheres is in feeling the natural way open to that way to thinking. Is the inside question reflected in the outside art of easy music or is the making of music about really feeling that is how I dance with the atmospheres I can hear it to move language in time. Making the language open we move to know in its doors of invitation pacing rallies of knowing really how people in

the world think and language in the back of my wanting
buttressing brain feels like a thinking explosion and old
ways look meek to me.

The Light without Reading Words

I am really thinking about underwater places others please with soft easy wanting now the pleasing ways. I am thinking about seeing and toward the depths of the water answers about ways that seeing moves with places of understanding. Water is about the ways that light plays with something. The water is itself and at the surface the light and ways water shines to easy move with playful sowing that lives in seeing. Water swallows ready passages that sail toward underwater places others want to see. The lights are easy on the surface. Questions about ways of seeing and the light that catches ideas thinking about how to see without light. Toward another seeing wanting torrents of sensing and lacking ways to easy see treats moving ideas with soft places of meanings. Water is time reading light into plates of the earth's feeling skin and ideas for future living together's question the seeing of the world that needs capture and light and eyes to see. That way ruptures the reason offering typing time to think with ways of moving and knowing with and without light.

The Storms of Diversity

The way of the storm is like a musician singing the persons of street walkers in the city that really jam the ways of thinking bringing the good music to the dance in the street. I think that a storm bathes the sounds of the music where one rains the ways getting the symphony of angry feelings that the world has right now and the sound can feel endearing at the same time. I think that the silly storm wants the world to listen to climate change about the ways if it makes the actual case rallying the people to think about changing our relationship with nature and I think the silliness of storms is the thinking that they will wake people up to change. Open the ways that you think about doing things and make time for thinking and learning diverse ways of movement and knowing and then in sheer bathing in the storm be like a very tiny raindrop. Open the ways that the storm teaches us to love the world and in that thinking fresh after storm awesome lush green of a new day languaging the calm pay attention to the way the sun gives in the life of everything. Languaging the ways of the storm rests in the open feelings of the waters pouring strong good slanting dances that are living in the sand of time and the sand answers the storm buttressing the feelings as the water moves it. Giving artful attention to real marks and streams in the sand shifts the thinking to not naming but naming patterns as good feeling movement that can't be described because naming a mark is not able to describe movement as it happens. In gale storms openings offer inspiration for possible forgiveness force of storms humble the good human if only for a schooling second. That forgiveness is a religious idea has nothing to do with the way I use it. It means that the earth is always trying to bathe the togetherness of all good things opening to possibilities for new ways. Thinking time is being together through the storms of change.

Floating

The patternings write full wanting inside words assigning matter to movements questions act within openings fun easy seeing words inside others. Flows that places wake inside the tremble of tired feelings soothe the ways of reasoning into ways of opening. Floating in easy flows of question. Walking I feel time in water places lying the flowing time walking paces the I that I am inside reading the ways places change. Easy flowering place places into dark deep ways withing the flows old toward nights that open into sprites that fun the floating eyes. The walking ways itself into the streams that place always fills with pattering lines of time that amaze the listener. Easying the pace is that opening that tired feelings please withing the pleasing walking into pleasing sooth. Good ways typing thanks the powers that always bring thinking to the floating ways to listen.

The Ripples

Have the desire to write about easy now of rippling patterns on the surface of the water. The water moves with the atmospheres managing open paces that bathe lines in it ways of movement that I feel as a gaming open person that by myself needs to face the many things that come at me amazing to understand the ways pacing dances the movement. Making the tone of managing really wants me to fight the drive to be monkey mind that races thinking gaming is about the way I dance the watery fluid environment favorite way is thinking and feeling like a not moving managing person but as a person ruddering the boat on the moving water. Is the way to make a dance with the engineering city keeping with the ways real people move or is the way we need to move making ways knowing that good people need more than fighting conditions of suffering in the city and can we language the ways water calms? Making the languaging that is having the dance of calm is the better way like making the sometimes space for autistic feeling that can introduce the ways water can think about how weak the cities are like feeling the ferocious hurricane. Pacing like the ripples is the way dance musics the city and the city paces open game by category four winds that destroy it and I think if we thought like the atmospheres we would think calming ways to be living. Like the atmospheres moving is all

about relation and I wonder if the ways dance my feelings
whereas knowing that the city dances to music of noise
we can't free ourselves feeling the faces is the gaze's game
that I try to play but the water dance suits me better.

Geyser

I want to write about easy gush of geyser and the pace beeing the ways under getting the easy water thinking to go up. Want to line the thinking about how important impulses breathe the liking of the places of typing really want to tell the reader how hard it is to have dances bringing so many invitations that sometimes I think that I am both a cave dweller and a geyser typing thinking feeling gaming ticcing climbing ringing in my thinking ears is the sound of gears furrowing underneath. The language of water is the pace of real thinking the water is the plastic morphing way potent making happens having the water is the source of gaming the space because water goes everywhere and it tries to speak the language of spaces that have the rallying relation with the art of arrangement and pattern and intensity. The gears are also the beeing that buzzes open spaces that are prized for making honey falling dropping from hives and is the geyser the pacing of the landing of thoughts that otherwise are in good chaotic form?

The Pace of Leurararara

I am thinking about making a language of my own and having that is going to change the feelings people think about when people want to teach about neurodiversity. Using the word we're answering the way things dance and the word of water I have today noises as fingering flings of passing getting the prancing water as leurararara. I leurararara the water between my fingers and easy is the dance. Paces of using a water source with my fingers forgets the time and opens my sanity gaming and playing atmosphere dances. I name sanity as using the things in the atmospheres to think and treat myself to calming things making the face of the demanding shoulds backing learning more calm. Demanding shoulds are behind every lesson. I mean the lessons of neurotypical teachers. The managing needs leurararara to move sometimes can be openings and sometimes seeing the water dance has knowings needing my attention in the water I can be calling a man of attention not distraction. The leurararara makes language in the repetition making our attention the way of the artful atmospheres and having that time to stim brings openings not closings rallying with atmospheres jams the music not the demands.

Underwater

In the underwater opens the silence where the pressure is peaceful unfeeling in calm thinking. I the greyish rallying being lose the colors of sound in the watered depths that rain the person of autism's dance to better the ease of perception. Perception is the way I sometimes think of the way I feel scans of the walking way is the feeling of fast language and pace of patterns that arouse my attention. The scans are the pace of the eyes preening the management of the peaceful resting thinking about where to walk. Is the underwater pacing the earth or is the earth pacing the underwater because I think that in that bathing dance that easy relations have both. In the underwater the peace is floating but the pace is bathing and seething.

I Language the Ways of the Currents Not the Ways of People

I want to write about the twallowing stick as the people's way of thinking about waves pacing to the water that is in my mind the way I see movements like the ways open water needs currents the same way I need heavy or easy feelings to move and I feel the coming cutting currents like the ways the language dances. The part I am thinking about is the walking too as the ways of pacing always in gaming the ways that the assembly paces liking the waves of the air that in the affect is languaging my difference as the peaceful and managing ways I can move and I don the dance piercing real buttressing paces of the city. The twallowing stick is the pace of cutting currents that I make the way I can walk and some people call this stimming that opens the much needed bathing in the space because if in the walks I don't have sticks I would not be able to move and the watchful real people would say how come the autistic man can't move? I feel that knowing about how I can calmly move when I twallow sticks is the way people will accept me the way open buttressing supporters do and I get price of languaging the each band of naming pace to think about the languaging orientation. I am banding language phrases to gether for people to come pacing my way people like metaphors people make meaning from them gathering language is putting the people together to understand. Open the language have the people gather its meaning the ability making the dance be an experiment. I think that to imagine new worlds is about the language orientation. People name things as the categories language can open that to be more attentive to how we are amazingly different the dances we open can jam the relation to not average answers not vox of voices that sound the same biting the autistic answers depriving us the right to language as we do.

Pace the Animal's Way

I want to write about the animals that are speaking the sensuous that is rallying the ways we need in the world and you want me to write about water wanting the calm and the storms of feeling but the animals know the atmospheres that are like water and that is the sensuous way of inside knowledge that is broken by words of science. Pace of sounds call artful attention to the ways we people back the words with meaning books that descend the meanings rather than the paces of rallying calm feelings and open the dome that is the bisophere to be the moving mind of making little patterns that most do not see when the words screen the makings to go to meaning. You are the word carer that names the experience and open that wanting way to more gaming the spaces of doing written work is like making managing of family of meanings the paces of life. The paces of life need paces of movement and color and sound and sitting to give more feeling to the world of life that every person needs to have empathy for the earth falling to the faces places of screens. The pace of the place we now live in is the way of each baptised word that is people's way of understanding it open the words picking the parts made by animals and plants and atmospheres and the words become the biosphere's music.

The Falling Pool of Time That Opens the Language of Autistic Life

I'm thinking about that amazing water in British Colum-bia and new waters that flood the land that watered as saturation and mud slides and how saturation can kill easily making teachings about the environment lan-guaged in ways people can understand because it feels tragic. Facing tragedy jams with triumph and the ways people might begin the managing of the earth better lan-guage of the back ground of the rallying earth will think more about how we need to go buttress the earth with bottom of getting to the point of support and feeling the language of the environment is the same as listening to my language. The pace of mud slides is the angry pain of the earth when people don't listen about climate change and that is the same as autistic anger and pain that exists in the really difficult world where big open ideas are talked about but leave autistic people out and I want to saturate this language so that making needing new paces can happen. That anger is about how people use the words we write but better famous people talk over us about autism and that brings us back to ignorance. Have the landings of the baptised language of the religious right-wing people rallying for rights to rape the language of autistic people in answers we don't consent or ruefully does the acceptance only come in the English language? The way of giving justice is the waters that wash away the language of paucity the language of falling the way leaves do. That falling gives us the freedom that we need to calmly go in the direction of the future.

The Inside of the Dark Sea

I want to have lots of language for water to day dancing the amazing depths of the sea pace imagines the dark weight of actual water having so much pressure that I am facing the appreciation calming pace gesturing the way of seeing the dark. The pressure is languaging the weight of the rolling wafting self that loses the feeling of I in the wallowing amazing depths that lots of life can not thrive by the weight and I am there underwater now. I am dark and heavy and feeling game of writing as real pressing pressure and although I am writing now I go to the dark floor of the sea to watch the way I am outside myself and yet inside the water. I talk about the water and the dark when I am really tired big ideas are making in the dark and I dance in the shadows where the body merges with the feelings of the earth and the sea and paces dreams support and the easy sun makes house of boundaries needing shadows to swallow the body people need to know how the easy relation works in the deep water really dark in the way that pace opens in the shadows. I think that real buttressing support is languaging the shadows that luster the real relation that has the meeting merging with the weight that lands language in the way mired thinking makes support myself having the wanting ways in which open shadows of the feelings make. Has the deep free thinking the sun or the shadows I think that the shadows spread over people the way water does and that is bathing the way I do in making meaning and languaging with the world. People are dancing in the sun of talking and using words my easy way is feeling the shared shadows the way like in the water and the dark gives a feeling of blending. Open share people have a way of good dancing and the language like talkers is like trying to swim but the leaves of words merge and dissolve in the water making the water and the leaves one. Knowing how to merge uses the bathing metaphor to feel the way aggregate of weight is the passive way to feel and answer the way of words but relation thinks about feeling the self wording face of being otherwise I would not be able to iterate myself without the feeling of weight padding me to know I am a language really want the people the talkers to think about weight and weightlessness. Peace as weight of the water a need for weight is the same as support that bathes in the weightlessness knowing that these dance aggregate of autistic bodies and languages the way wanting deeds of weak writing to underestimate the way of meaning and autsitic love of managing in the dark. Autistic love opens the language of support to be thinking about weight somehow feeling as gearing in the water to go to the typing when it feels merging with the atmospheres can you dig it.

Digging for Water

Please try and tell me is the difference between digging and pacing all that different other than the managing versus the making and I feel there is similarity in the way pace is lining toward the forging water the way we try to find it underground. I think that the difference between digging and languaging pace is like the difference between having tired water that pools versus the water that flows lucky you have the ability the way of talking but I have the ability here in naming much effort in my finger as the very buttress of the feeling body that bathes in desire and pace is about not having to dig but about having to forge the way feeling the flow the way managing and making work together. I have that answer because I want to make some kind of understanding about how typing works ceaselessly wanting to here be in the moment of dancing many thoughts are the people who talk answering the way of questions fast because giving answers is easy or because answering is expected. I am thinking that knowing things comes that way of feeling managing and making together and that tentative way of candid discussion is the water ceaselessly freeing the facts from the rocks of fears that are starting naming Omicron actual virus of Corona and in that I want to discuss the ways of talking as speculation. Talking is easy and assumes that we know but it has also this uncertainty understanding that we do not know. The Omicron virus is the water of mutation and I the Adam game the words and the woulds the way water flows. The game and the speculation are each in this way crevicing the way facing the water's nexus faces the rocks and that necessary making is to have the understanding of the mass speculation knowing the thinking of the game's watery answers. Waters of speculation at the nexus are the paces I dance every day.

Pacing the Thanks

I would like to thank the ways of water and the people who always manage to saturate ideas, with people like Aviv Nisinzweig who brings my work and world to live in and Erin Manning who buttresses words musical and magical thinking and my mom Estée Klar for supporting my ideas with art and languaging relation and want the dad Henry Wolfond of amazing support to have acknowledgment and punctum books calling for the works of buttressing neurodiversity and Chris Martin and Ciragh Lyons and Veronica MacLeod and Ellen Bleiwas and dis assembly in rallying and making this like a book of gateways opening for others to offer a new way of being to gether for creating paces that are needed for neurodiversity to live.

I want to thank all the readers who will share the ideas in the future dancing diversity.

Printed in Poland
by Amazon Fulfillment
Poland Sp. z o.o., Wrocław

26290966R00058